BECOMING
A WOMAN OF
FAITH

BECOMING
A WOMAN OF
FAITH

CYNTHIA HEALD

THOMAS NELSON PUBLISHERS
Nashville

Published in association with the literary agency of Alive Communications, 7680 Goddard Street, Suite #200, Colorado Springs, CO 80920.

Published in Nashville, Tennessee, by Thomas Nelson, Inc.

Scripture quotations noted NASB are from the NEW AMERICAN STANDARD BIBLE®, © Copyright The Lockman Foundation 1960, 1962, 1963, 1968, 1971, 1972, 1973, 1975, 1977. Used by permission.

Scripture quotations noted NKJV are from THE NEW KING JAMES VER-SION. Copyright © 1979, 1980, 1982, Thomas Nelson, Inc., Publishers.

Scripture quotations noted NLT are from the *Holy Bible,* New Living Translation, copyright © 1996. Used by permission of Tyndale House Publishers, Inc., Wheaton, Illinois 60189. All rights reserved.

Scripture quotations noted THE MESSAGE are from *The Message: in Contemporary English.* Copyright © 1993 by Eugene H. Peterson.

Scripture quotations noted AMPLIFIED are from THE AMPLIFIED BIBLE: Old Testament. Copyright © 1962, 1964 by Zondervan Publishing House (used by permission); and from THE AMPLIFIED NEW TESTAMENT. Copyright © 1958 by the Lockman Foundation (used by permission).

ISBN 0-7852-7244-5

Printed in the United States of America

6   05 04 03 02 01

Contents

How to Use This Guide

❦

This Bible study has been created to help you search the Scriptures and draw closer to God as you seek to grow in your understanding and practice of faith. All you need is a Bible, a writing tool, and an expectant heart. You may find it helpful, however, to have access to supplemental resources such as a general dictionary, a general Bible commentary, a Bible handbook, or a study Bible with reference notations.

Becoming a Woman of Faith is appropriate for individual as well as group use, and for women of any age and season of life. Before you begin each chapter, pray for attentiveness to how God is speaking to you through His Word and for sensitivity to His prompting. At the conclusion of each chapter, you will have the opportunity to write out a favorite Scripture verse from the study passages. As you meditate on and pray over this personal selection, ask God to use it in strengthening your faith. Adding Scripture memory to this practice will help you abide in Christ day by day as His truth dwells deep within your mind and heart.

Quotations from Christian writers have been selected to help you understand the biblical content of each chapter and to enhance your personal response to God's Word. Consider using the "Notes" section in the back of this book as a resource list for further devotional reading and study.

The Bible has much to say about the importance of learning from and encouraging one another in the community of believers. If you are using this study with a small group, the questions and exercises will give you excellent opportunities for talking and praying together about deepening your trust in the faithfulness of God.

$\mathcal{P}$REFACE

If faith means trusting in something we can't absolutely know or prove is true, then to varying degrees everyone exercises faith in daily life. Without faith that there is a purpose for our lives beyond immediate circumstances, life will ultimately seem empty and meaningless.

Faith entails complete confidence in its object. It is a strong conviction that what we believe is worthy of our trust. When I place my faith in another person, I trust that he will be true to his character and promises. Life continually confronts us with decision points in which we must choose where and in whom we will place our trust. In a world busily promoting every kind of belief system, it is crucial that we seek diligently for the most trustworthy object of our faith.

In *Becoming a Woman of Faith*, you will have opportunity to consider scriptural truths regarding the love and faithfulness of God. Your initial response of faith in accepting God's gift of salvation propels you on a journey to the highest and best. But this faith is not limited to a one-time encounter with the Lord. Because of God's faithfulness, your trust can grow and bear the fruit of a vibrant, living faith. True faith will undergird your decisions and actions; it will shield you from the enemy; it will empower your prayers; and it will enable you to withstand testing, temptations— and even your doubts.

One of the highlights of this study for me was the in-depth look at the lives of those saints listed in the Hall of Faith in Hebrews 11. I was greatly challenged by how these men and women were willing to move to unknown places, risk danger in hiding enemy spies, and brave imprisonment and destitution— all because of the One in whom they placed their trust. I will revisit again and again these courageous heroes whose faith enabled them to live and die for God.

This study has changed me, renewed me, and encouraged me to keep growing in my faith and to keep walking by faith. Understanding that my faith can deepen and become more precious has drawn me closer to the Lord and given me much hope. I have a new sense of God's commitment to me and a fresh confidence that I can run this race faithfully.

My prayer for you is that your faith will increase and be strengthened. May your life be one of wholehearted trust in our God, who above all is faithful and righteous in all His dealings. In His priceless and abounding love for you, He desires your trust. God's richest blessing on you as you become a woman of faith.

Love in Christ,

Cynthia Heald

CHAPTER 1

The Faithfulness of God

❦

Through the LORD's mercies we are not
   consumed,
Because His compassions fail not.
They are new every morning;
Great is Your faithfulness.

Lamentations 3:22–23 NKJV

Upon God's faithfulness rests our whole hope of future blessedness. Only as He is faithful will His covenants stand and His promises be honored. Only as we have complete assurance that He is faithful may we live in peace and look forward with assurance to the life to come . . . The tempted, the anxious, the fearful, the discouraged may all find new hope and good cheer in the knowledge that our Heavenly Father is faithful.[1]

A. W. Tozer

*C*omprehending the faithfulness of God is crucial to becoming a woman of faith. How can we have a vital faith in someone we're not sure is faithful? I like Proverbs 25:19: "Confidence in an unfaithful man in time of trouble is like a bad tooth and a foot out of joint" (NKJV). This Scripture vividly describes the distressing results and disappointment of misplaced faith.

The recipient of our faith often determines the measure of our faith. The Hebrew word for *faith* is *ëmûnâh*, which means "firmness, steadiness."[2] This word is used to describe the absolute dependability of God's character. Because God is firm and steady, you can put your weight on Him. He will hold you securely and steadfastly.

God Is Faithful

1. God's trustworthy character is acknowledged, praised, and extolled all through Scripture. How does each of the following passages describe His faithfulness?

a. Deuteronomy 32:4

b. Psalm 36:5

c. Psalm 119:90, 138

d. Hebrews 10:23

e. Hebrews 13:8

2. In Psalm 89, Ethan the Ezrahite affirms God's faithfulness. Based upon how the psalmist described God in Psalm 89:1–8, how would you explain that God is trustworthy?

———————————— ————————————

Upon God's faithfulness rests our whole hope of future blessedness. Only as He is faithful will His covenants stand and His promises be honored. Only as we have complete assurance that He is faithful may we live in peace and look forward with assurance to the life to come.[3]

A. W. Tozer

———————————— ————————————

God's Faithfulness Is Active

3. God demonstrates His faithfulness to us in many ways. What specific aspects of our lives do the following verses address?

a. 1 Corinthians 1:4–9 (See also Phil. 1:3–6.)

b. 1 Corinthians 10:13

c. Hebrews 13:5–6

d. 1 John 1:9

The puritan preacher Thomas Lye remarked that in this passage [Heb. 13:5] the Greek has five negatives and may thus be rendered, "I will not, not leave thee; neither will I not, not forsake thee." Five times God emphasized to us that He will not forsake us. He wants us to firmly grasp the truth that whatever circumstances may indicate, we must believe, on the basis of His promise, that He has not forsaken us or left us to the mercy of those circumstances.[4]

Jerry Bridges

4. Moses, the psalmists, and the disciples all testify of God's steadfastness. What is one specific way in which you have experienced the faithfulness of God in your life?

God's Faithfulness Is Unconditional

5. The psalmist Ethan the Ezrahite specifically wrote of God's unfailing commitment in the covenant He made with David. What can you observe about God's faithfulness from Psalm 89:30–37?

6. The Lord spoke clearly and directly concerning His covenant. How does this scriptural affirmation of God's steadfast commitment help you in an area in which you have trouble trusting God?

Man fails in all points, but God in none. To be faithful is one of the eternal characteristics of God, in which he always places a great part of his glory: his

truth is one of his peculiar treasures and crown jewels, and he will never endure that it should be tarnished in any degree.[5]

Charles Spurgeon

Author's Reflection

Although it has been many years now, I still remember how my husband and I would encourage our children to jump from the edge of the swimming pool into our arms. It was truly a leap of faith for them to go into unknown waters, trusting in our love and strength to catch them. "Come on, I'm here. I promise I won't let you go under—I'll grab you. It's fun! You'll like it." Sometimes the assurances took a long time before the first jump. Inevitably, after the initial leap, there would be squeals of delight over repeated jumps along with pleas for "one more time."

In a similar way, our Father stands with open arms and asks us to trust in His faithfulness to hold us and keep us from "going under." Truly, He is steady, and He firmly grasps us as we reach out to Him. We can rest our whole weight upon Him, confident that He will never forsake us.

Who else can we trust so implicitly? Who else extends unconditional love and faithfulness? Who else offers the surety of unfailing love, which is new every morning? Who else calls us to an abandoned trust with the assurance that we will never be abandoned? He alone is worthy to hear, "Great is Your faithfulness!"

Strengthening Your Faith

Choose a Scripture from this chapter that particularly assures you of God's faithfulness. Meditate upon it and write it down, either in your own words (you may find it helpful to use a dictionary, and to look up the verse in another translation, for suggestions in rewriting it) or by personalizing it with your name and personal pronouns. You might feel prompted to write the verse as a special word from the Lord just to you. Throughout this week, pray over your verse to help strengthen your faith.

To help you get started, here is an example I created from Hebrews 13:5–6:

I, as your Father, want you to be content with what you have. In fact, what you have is Me! And, contrary to material things, I will always be with you. I will never abandon you. Put your faith in Me. Don't be afraid of anyone, because I am your helper and faithful Father.

❧Scripture Memory

Lamentations 3:22–23, or the verse(s) you chose to strengthen your faith.

CHAPTER 2

ℰNCOUNTERING 𝒟OUBT

The father instantly replied, "I do believe, but help me not to doubt!"

Mark 9:24 NLT

Doubt is a word that strikes terror to the soul and often it is suppressed in a way that is very unhealthy. This is a particularly acute problem for those who have been reared in Christian homes and in the Christian Church. From their earliest years they have accepted the facts of Christianity solely on the basis of confidence and trust in parents, friends, and minister. As the educational process develops, a re-examination of their position takes place. This is a healthy and necessary experience to bring virile faith into being.[1]

Paul Little

he desperate father of a son possessed by an evil spirit begged Jesus to do something if He could. "What do you mean, '*If* I can'?" Jesus replied. "Anything is possible if a person believes." Then the father answered honestly by pleading, "I do believe, but help me not to doubt." On another occasion the disciples said to the Lord, "We need more faith; tell us how to get it" (Luke 17:5 NLT). Uncertainty in our faith is an issue to recognize and address, not to ignore. To help us in times of doubt, we have two excellent prayers recorded in Scripture from Jesus' encounters with the grieving father and the disciples—"Help me" and "Teach me." At one point even John the Baptist needed reassurance that Christ was the Savior, as did Thomas. Reading about some of the renowned "doubters" in Scripture and studying Jesus' responses to them will give us insight, encouragement, and guidance as we encounter doubt in the life of faith.

Doubters of the Bible

1. A good working definition of *doubt* can help us understand how to grow in faith. Use a dictionary or thesaurus, and write out your definition of *doubt*.

2. The Bible realistically portrays those who have doubted God— some honestly, some rebelliously. Read the following Scriptures and identify the doubter(s), the circumstances triggering their doubt, and the consequences or results of their doubt.

a. Deuteronomy 1:19–36

b. Mark 9:14–27

c. Luke 7:18–28

d. John 20:24–29

A doubting temper, fond of dwelling on difficulties and objections, is fatal to unity of mind, heart, and will. Doubts, if they assail you, are neither to be timidly shrunk from nor idly played with, but honestly faced and fought. But the grand secret of conviction is to dwell first and constantly on the *positive evidence* of truth. If that is adequate, unanswerable, then a thousand questions we cannot at present answer need not

trouble us. They can wait; but *facts* will not wait. Here
is a great secret, not only of *strength*, but of *rest*. And
in rest is a reservoir of energy.[2]

E. R. Conder and W. Clarkson

3. The Scriptures you just studied tell of Israel's doubting God's wisdom in going into Canaan; of a hopeful yet hesitant father in desperate need; of John the Baptist's questioning of the man at the very center of his life; of Thomas's insistence on seeing for himself. Which of these instances most describe the doubts in your life (past or present)? Why?

4. Read Psalm 77, in which Asaph expressed profound doubts about the faithfulness of God. Why was he in such anguish, and how did he find relief?

Is there trouble in your life? Do you feel God has let
you down? Then do what the psalmist did: review evi-
dences of God's loving-kindness and care to you.

Begin with Calvary and move to your personal life. Then say, "Lord, that's who You've always been, that's who You are according to the testimony of my friends, that's who You are according to the testimony of the many people who've gone on before. I trust You to be my help now." This is faith. Our faith is nourished by developing a strong sense of God's acting in the past, so that we begin to count on Him to act consistently with His character in the future—again, and again, and again.[3]

C. Donald Cole

A Little Faith

5. The disciples suffered from doubt, especially during storms. As you read these verses, write down the circumstances, the disciple(s)' response, the Lord's action, and the ultimate lesson they learned.

    a. Matthew 14:22–33

    b. Luke 8:22–25

6. In each of these passages you just read, Jesus reproved the disciples for their doubt and lack of faith. Why do you think the

Lord used these startling situations to point out their "little" faith?

Faith may be true, and yet weak; at first, like a grain of mustard-seed. Peter had faith enough to bring him upon the water, yet, because not enough to carry him through, Christ tells him he had but *little*. Our discouraging doubts and fears are all owing to the weakness of our faith: *therefore we doubt,* because we are but *of little faith* . . . They knew before that he was the Son of God, but now they know it better. Faith, after a conflict with unbelief, is sometimes the more active, and gets to greater degrees of strength by being exercised. Now they *know it of a truth.*[4]

Matthew Henry

Author's Reflection

My greatest moments of doubt come when I question God's ways. Pain, suffering, and trials will always be in my life and in the lives of those I love. God challenges me to keep going into a land flowing with milk and honey, but there are still giants to contend with. In my "little" faith I doubt the goodness and faithfulness of the Lord. I believe that He is always with me, but when the winds begin to whip up the waves, I cry out for the Lord to wake up.

How quickly I forget, as did the disciples, that Jesus told them as they entered the boat, "Let us cross over to the other side of the lake." It was a promise from Him that they *were going to the other side!* I need not doubt His word, no matter what the circumstances.

After Asaph cried out, "Has God forgotten to be gracious?" he *remembered* the Lord's work and wonders of old. He recalled God's faithfulness, and it was enough. This is *faith*—trusting God with my past, present, and future even though, logically, I should trust no one but myself.

But if I do rely on my own insight, I will spend my life risking nothing, depending only on what I can see and touch. I will be my own rescuer. I will listen to my doubts, debate God's ways, and cling to my own understanding—and suffer the consequences of these choices by dwelling in the wilderness, living in fear, and going under in the storm.

It is not wrong to doubt, but it is wrong not to deal with our doubts before God. Asaph, John the Baptist, Thomas, and Peter—each in his own way cried out, "Lord, save me!" And immediately, "Jesus stretched out His hand and caught him."

In dealing with the arrogant asserter of doubt, it is not the right method to tell him to stop doubting. It

is rather the right method to tell him to go on doubting, to doubt a little more, to doubt every day newer
and wilder things in the universe, until at last, by
some strange enlightenment, he may begin to doubt
himself.[5]

G. K. Chesterton

❧

Strengthening Your Faith

Choose a Scripture from this chapter that can encourage you
when you encounter doubt. Meditate upon it and write it down
either in your own words (a dictionary and a second translation
could help you here), personalize it with your name, or simply
write it out in your favorite version as a special word from the
Lord to you. Throughout this week, pray over your verse to help
you turn to the Lord when you encounter doubt.

❧Scripture Memory
Mark 9:24, or the verse(s) you chose to strengthen your faith.

CHAPTER 3

THE GIFT OF GOD

❦

*For by grace you have been saved through
faith, and that not of yourselves; it is the gift
of God, not of works, lest anyone should boast.*

Ephesians 2:8–9 NKJV

Faith is the hand of the heart which receives salvation.[1]
R. M. Edgar

*I*n order for a gift truly to be given, it must be received. Without the recipient's acceptance and acknowledgment, the gift is, in effect, an offer. God has freely extended the gift of salvation, but it can be accepted only by faith. The grace of God offers forgiveness, a new life, adoption into God's family, and eternal life in Christ Jesus. As overwhelming and priceless as it is, however, this gift is not forced upon us. God purchased our salvation through the sacrifice of His Son on the cross for "whoever believes" (John 3:16 NKJV). Oswald Chambers defined *believe* as "literally to commit . . . To be 'a believer in Jesus' means to bank our confidence in Him, to stake our soul upon His honor."[2] How precious is the grace of God in the hour we first believe—and what a joy to continue with trust, conviction, reliance, dependence, and confidence as we live in the acceptance of His grace.

The Gift of Salvation

1. Understanding that salvation is truly a gift is key to understanding the nature of faith. What do the following Scriptures teach about this extravagant gift?

    a. Romans 5:6–11

    b. Romans 6:23

c. Ephesians 2:8–9

2. The apostle Paul wrote passionately that we are justified by faith, not by deeds of the law. How did he describe our standing with God in the following passages?

a. Romans 1:16–17

b. Romans 3:21–26

c. Romans 5:1–2

d. Romans 9:30–33

❧

The apostle was justified in his boasting in the gospel, because of the high end it was the means of securing—nothing less than the salvation of men. This salvation it is his aim, in the Epistle, to set in its true light. It is a moral, a spiritual deliverance; an enfranchisement of the soul; an opening of the prison doors; a healing radical, thorough, and lasting. A righteous

God can only be reconciled with sinful, disobedient men by communicating to them his own righteousness. The inner nature, the spiritual being, the moral character, is the sphere of the great salvation which Christ brings, which the gospel announces . . . Like his Divine Master, Paul insisted strenuously upon the importance, the necessity of faith. This is a sign of the spirituality of our religion, which begins with the heart, and works from within outwardly. But Scripture gives no countenance to the mystical doctrine that faith is a mere sentiment, having no definite object. On the contrary, it reveals God and his promises, and especially his Son and the truth relating to him, as the objects of faith.[3]

J. Radford Thomson

The Response of Faith

3. God has lovingly imparted His salvation and righteousness to us. How do these passages teach us to respond to such a gift?

   a. Mark 10:13–16

   b. John 1:10–13

4.Jesus was displeased with the disciples for rebuking those who brought their children to be with Him. Why do you think He taught us to receive His kingdom as a little child?

5. Abraham is our example of receiving the gift of righteousness by faith. Read Romans chapter 4 and study Paul's argument that Abraham was justified by faith, not by his obedience to the law.

    a. What was Paul's declaration in 4:1–5?

    b. Summarize the distinction Paul made in verses 13–16 between law and faith in our standing before God.

    c. In 4:17–25, how did Paul use Abraham's example to explain our relationship to God?

This way of glorifying God by a firm reliance on his bare promise was so very agreeable to God's design,

and so very conducive to his honour, that he graciously accepted it as a righteousness, and justified him though there was not that in the thing itself which could merit such an acceptance. This shows why faith is chosen to be the prime condition of our justification, because it is a grace that of all others gives glory to God.[4]

Matthew Henry

6. Romans 10:17 tells us that faith comes by hearing and hearing by the Word of God. Describe your own experience of hearing the Word of God and responding in faith to God's gift.

Author's Reflection

I received God's gift of salvation when I was twelve years old. In answer to our pastor's question if I believed that Jesus was the Son of God and that He died for my sins, I gave a heartfelt, "Yes, I do." I believed firmly in God's love—after all, He had sent His

Son to die for me. I knew that if He loved me so much, then I could trust Him implicitly. I certainly didn't understand that I had been justified by faith or that righteousness had been imputed to me, but I believed—I had faith in the living God. My beginning with the Lord was with a child's understanding, but the faith was real nevertheless, and it has stayed real for fifty years.

Often, when I consider the incredible grace of the Lord in His offer of forgiveness, freedom, and rest, I am overwhelmed by His love and goodness. How could I *not* trust One who loved me so much that He gave His only Son in order that I, too, could become His child? It is a high privilege for me to place my confidence in Him and stake my soul upon His honor.

I love the hymn "My Faith Has Found a Resting Place." In particular, the second verse expresses the response of my heart in faith to God's offer of grace:

> Enough for me that Jesus saves,
> This ends my fear and doubt;
> A sinful soul I come to Him,
> He will not cast me out.
> I need no other evidence,
> I need no other plea;
> It is enough that Jesus died
> And rose again for me.[5]

Strengthening Your Faith

Choose a Scripture from this chapter that is especially important to you in expressing God's gift of salvation. As a way of acknowledging this gift, write it out (from your favorite translation, in your own words, or by personalizing it) and meditate on it. Throughout this week, pray and rejoice over your verse as an expression of your faith.

❧Scripture Memory
Ephesians 2:8–9 or the verse(s) you chose to strengthen your faith.

CHAPTER 4

$\mathcal{F}$AITH IN $\mathcal{A}$CTION

❧

But without faith it is impossible to please
Him, for he who comes to God must believe
that He is, and that He is a rewarder of those
who diligently seek Him.

Hebrews 11:6 NKJV

Now, if faith is the gaze of the heart at God, and if this
gaze is but the raising of the inward eyes to meet the
all-seeing eyes of God, then it follows that it is one of
the easiest things possible to do. It would be like God
to make the most vital thing easy and place it within
the range of possibility for the weakest and poorest of
us.[1]

A. W. Tozer

*B*efore coming to faith in God, our only options for trust are in ourselves or in others. Trust and confidence are necessary for growth in any relationship. And so it is in our relationship with God. We cannot know the Lord or ever hope to please Him without faith. But unlike trust within a human context, our faith in God will never be disappointed. It is rooted in God's gift of salvation, freely offered so that we can experience life as His children. As we shift our belief system from confidence in the flesh (ourselves and others) to confidence in Him, we are able to enter fully into a rich communion that rewards us with the deepening discovery of God's faithfulness. As we put faith into action, we demonstrate to God that we do believe in Him—and receive confirmation that He responds to those who seek Him diligently.

Stepping Out in Faith

1. John records in his gospel an instance in which people sought out Jesus to ask Him a crucial question. Read this exchange in John 6:28–37, noticing especially what Jesus said in verses 29–30 and 36. What did Jesus want them to understand?

The work of faith is the work of God. They enquire after the *works* of God, (in the plural number), being

careful about *many things;* but Christ directs them to one work, which includes all, the one thing needful; that *you believe*, which supersedes all the works of the *ceremonial law;* the work which is necessary to the acceptance of all the other works, and which produces them, for without faith it is impossible to please God.[2]

Matthew Henry

2. The Israelites in the wilderness demonstrated how a lack of faith can displease God. In Psalm 78 Asaph recounts how Israel believed in God, yet they did not act on their faith. Read verses 12–39 and describe how the Israelites specifically failed to exercise faith, and how God responded.

3. In Psalm 78, Asaph observed that despite the marvelous things God did for Israel, still they demanded proof that God was faithful. When you find yourself in the wilderness, in what ways do you tend to test God or trust in Him?

Our Actions, God's Response

4. By faith we believe that God honors those who seek Him. In each of the following passages, describe how each individual exercised faith and what happened as a result.

a. Luke 7:1–10

b. Acts 3:1–16

5. It is encouraging to read in the Scriptures of miraculous healings, but in practice it is not always so easy or comfortable to demonstrate our faith. The Bible records the stories of those whose faith endured under extreme pressures. What do you observe about how faith was expressed and honored in the circumstances recounted here?

a. Daniel 3:8–30

b. Daniel 6:1–23

c. 2 Timothy 4:9–18

6. In this chapter you have studied all kinds of circumstances in which people were asked to exercise their faith. What have you learned about faith, and how God rewards it, that is meaningful for your life with God?

Author's Reflection

The year was 1974. My husband, Jack, and I were fervently praying to know the Lord's will. Should Jack sell his veterinary practice in order for us to move to San Antonio and receive training with a lay Christian organization called The Navigators? For the past ten years we had been living very happily in Temple,

Texas. We had four children, a nice home, plenty of friends, and a comfortable income. It seemed that the Lord was leading us to leave all this, but we weren't sure!

In the process we sought counsel, which was helpful but not definitive in setting direction. We asked for some "sign" that would let us know what to do, but there was no specific indicator. We could see pros and cons on both sides, and we were truly committed to choosing the Lord's will, not our own. Still, it was not clear which choice God wanted us to make.

I will never forget that night when we were talking and praying, trying to reach a decision. Finally, Jack said, "Hebrews 11:6— 'without faith it is impossible to please [God].' I think we have to take the first step of faith and trust God to lead us or close the door. Let's go to San Antonio this week to check on schools and the availability of houses to rent. We'll go by faith and trust God to show us His will."

As we took steps through opening doors, it became clear to us that it was God's will for us to make the move. However, the fact that we moved was not the most important issue. The significance of this story is that we had to exercise our faith. Although it was not a life-threatening trial like walking into a lion's den or a fiery furnace, it represented a tremendous upheaval in our lives. Were we willing to move on faith, and faith alone? Were we even willing to "spy out the land"? This episode was God's way of teaching us to put faith in action, increasing our dependence on Him, and deepening our trust.

I learned in that event what I have experienced over and over again since: Any time we exercise our faith, no matter what our circumstances, God Himself becomes our reward.

———————————— ❧ ————————————

Assurance of faith is never gained by reserve, but only by abandonment.[3]

Oswald Chambers

———————————— ❧ ————————————

Strengthening Your Faith

Choose a Scripture from this chapter that impresses you concerning the importance of acting in faith. Meditate on it as you paraphrase it in your own words, or personalize it with your name, or simply write it out in your favorite translation as a special word from the Lord just to you. Throughout this week, pray over your verse to help strengthen your faith in anticipation of God's gracious response.

❧Scripture Memory
Hebrews 11:6, or the verse(s) you chose to strengthen your faith.

CHAPTER 5

Walking by Faith

For we walk by faith [we regulate our lives
and conduct ourselves by our conviction or
belief respecting man's relationship to God
and divine things, with trust and holy fervor;
thus we walk] not by sight or appearance.

2 Corinthians 5:7 AMPLIFIED

Faith is for this world, and sight is reserved for the other
world: and it is our duty, and will be our interest, to
walk by faith, till we come to live by sight.[1]

Matthew Henry

I like Matthew Henry's thought that faith is for this world and sight is for heaven. While we are here, we must exercise our faith and live for the eternal—the reality we cannot see now. This world is not our home; our citizenship is in heaven. We are pilgrims on a journey through a world that entices and tempts its travelers to neglect the eternal. Therefore, we must travel with faith in the Lord, who wants to lead us through to our eternal home. Since we can't trust our sight, we must learn to walk by faith. To live this way requires that we cast our weight fully on the Faithful One, seeking to live by the values of His kingdom. The more we surrender our desire to walk by sight, the deeper our trust grows. We will begin to experience the freedom of living by faith. More and more, we will be able to turn away from the ways of the world and fix our eyes on Jesus.

Living by Faith

1. Once we receive the gift of God through faith, our whole life is transformed. How do these Scriptures describe the changed life of one who lives by faith?

    a. 2 Corinthians 5:12–21

b. Galatians 2:20

c. Galatians 6:14

d. Ephesians 2:19–22

2. Paul provided glimpses of his journey of faith in his letters to the churches. Read the following passages and summarize how Paul lived his life of faith.
    a. 2 Corinthians 12:7–10

b. Philippians 3:1–14

c. 2 Timothy 4:6–8

No longer will I be concerned about what self wants, but about what Christ wants. When I pray I will not always be asking for things for my comfort and convenience but rather I will be seeking a place in God's will and asking for grace to stand where God wants me. I will not strive to show my love for God by the efforts of the flesh, but rather by the worship and trust of my heart. I will no longer try to show what great things I can do for Him, but will yield myself to Him so that He can show the world what great things He can do for me.[2]

Buell H. Kazee

Living for the Eternal

3. Living by faith means a commitment to living for the eternal—God's kingdom. What do these verses teach about the importance of living for what endures?

a. 1 Corinthians 3:9–15

b. 2 Corinthians 4:16–18

c. Colossians 3:1–4

4. Jesus taught that we are *in* but not *of* the world. How do the following passages help you understand the dangers of worldly entanglements?

a. Mark 4:18–19

b. 1 John 2:15–16

5. Because we are in the world, it is easy to become entangled. What tends to hinder you from keeping an eternal perspective?

---   ---

And Paul here has stated the true secret of bearing trials with patience. It is to look at the things which are unseen. To anticipate the glories of the heavenly

world. To fix the eye on the eternal happiness which is beyond the grave; and to reflect how short these trials *are*, compared with the eternal glories of heaven; and how short they will *seem* to be when we are there.[3]

Albert Barnes

6. Few people have actually seen the unseen world. The prophet Elisha was able to give his servant a glimpse of the eternal. Read 2 Kings 6:8–23 and explain what gave Elisha the confidence to walk by faith.

No wonder that, in this moment of apparent danger, Elisha was full of calm trust. Knowing Benhadad's designs, he might have escaped had he desired, but with the forces of the invisible King interposed between him and his enemies, he did not feel even this to be necessary. Not less confidently, in seasons of danger from ungodly men, may the believer commit his way unto the Lord. It may not be given him to see the symbols of invisible protection, but not the less surely can he depend that "the angel of the Lord encampeth round

about them that fear him, and delivereth them" (Ps. 34:7). He can say with David, "I will not be afraid of ten thousand of people that have set themselves against me round about" (Ps. 3:6). They can do him no further harm than God sees meet to allow. They that are for him are more than they that be against him.[4]

J. Orr

7. God does not leave us helpless. He promises to be our shield and defender as we live in the world. Consider those such as Elisha who have faced down armies, or others who have been thrown into fiery furnaces and lions' dens. How do their experiences encourage your walk of faith?

Author's Reflection

Lorne Sanny, a past president of The Navigators, shared a story of how many years earlier he had been taking his young son on a walk. The little boy was running ahead of him, looking at rocks and bugs, when suddenly a large dog appeared on the trail. Lorne's son came running back to him, wide-eyed, and immediately grabbed his father's hand. Then he turned back around and said bravely, "Hi, big dog!"[5]

This is a good illustration of walking by faith. As a new creation in Christ, I can take hold of His hand and walk confidently through the world. It doesn't mean that I will not have to face lions, fiery furnaces, or armies, but I do not have to fear them. My faith is in the living God, and my life is hidden with Christ. In reality, the unseen world is more real than the seen, for the world will one day pass away. Eternity is forever.

True faith transforms us and imparts courage. We can live with conviction and hope because our God is all-powerful and completely trustworthy. We can sing with David:

> I love you, LORD; you are my strength.
> The LORD is my rock, my fortress, and my
>   savior;
>   my God is my rock, in whom I find protection.
>   He is my shield, the strength of my salvation,
>   and my stronghold.
> I will call on the LORD, who is worthy of praise,
>   for he saves me from my enemies.
>
> *Psalm 18:1–3* NLT

Strengthening Your Faith

Choose a Scripture from this chapter that helps you understand what it means to walk by faith. Write it out here from your favorite translation, in your own words, or by personalizing it, and meditate on it. Throughout this week, pray over your verse as a way of helping yourself focus on what is eternally significant.

ℰ Scripture Memory

Second Corinthians 5:7, or the verse(s) you chose to strengthen your faith.

$\mathcal{T}$HE $\mathcal{S}$HIELD OF $\mathcal{F}$AITH

*In every battle you will need faith as your
shield to stop the fiery arrows aimed at you
by Satan.*

Ephesians 6:16 NLT

The shield was an ingenious device by which blows and arrows might be parried off, and the whole body defended. It could be made to protect the head, or the heart, or thrown behind to meet an attack there. As long as the soldier had his shield, he felt secure; and as long as a Christian has faith, he is safe. It comes to his aid in every attack that is made on him, no matter from what quarter; it is the defense and guardian of every other Christian grace; and it secures the protection which the Christian needs in the whole of the spiritual war.[1]

Albert Barnes

*K*nowing the warfare we must face as His children, God has given each of us a suit of armor as protection against Satan's attacks. We are to put on the full armor of God so that we can stand firm against the devil's schemes, but for our purposes of studying faith we will focus on the shield. The soldier's shield Paul had in mind when he used this analogy was large, approximately two-and-a-half by four feet, and shaped like an oblong door. Made of leather, it could be soaked in water to fireproof it, ensuring that fiery darts could not harm the soldier who used it properly. The New American Standard Bible emphasizes, "*in addition to all,* taking up the shield of faith with which you will be able to extinguish all the flaming missiles of the evil one" (Eph. 6:16, emphasis added). Our faith is essential protection, battle-proofed by a loving God who has already overcome the world. All we have to do is pick up the shield.

The Safety of Faith

1. Once we are born of God, we have an enemy who continually seeks to defeat us. What do the following passages teach about living victoriously in the world?

    a. Ephesians 6:14–17

    b. 1 Peter 5:8–9

c. 1 John 5:4–5

2. As a young shepherd, David was appalled at how Goliath, the heathen Philistine, was taunting the Israelites—and getting away with it! This giant may have intimidated the Israeli soldiers, but not David. Find out what happened in 1 Samuel 17:45–51, and describe how David wielded the shield of faith.

David's contest with Goliath will only be apprehended in its true light if the latter be regarded as a representative of the world, and David the representative of the Church.[2]

E. W. Hengstenberg

3. Paul wrote in 2 Corinthians 10:4, "We use God's mighty weapons, not mere worldly weapons, to knock down the Devil's strongholds" (NLT). In the following verses, how did the psalmists express their faith in God's protection?

a. Psalm 3:1–4

b. Psalm 18:1–3

c. Psalm 84:10–12

4. A good antidote for the battle-weary is renewed conviction that God is committed to being our shield. What do these Scriptures teach concerning our part in receiving His protection?

a. Psalm 91:1–4

b. Psalm 119:10–11

c. Ephesians 6:10–13

For it is God's Word which teaches us how to put on Christ and His graces so that we are fitly armed. Never flatter yourself into thinking you can do without this priceless book. We have all known those who content themselves with a profession of Christ and

a smattering of gifts and works, and do not wish to know if there is more to the Christian life. They are the ones whose graces freeze when winter winds buffet their souls. But the saint whose faith has been insulated from error by the truth of the gospel will be able to withstand all Satan's icy blasts.[3]

William Gurnall

Dealing with Danger

5. In the face of conflict and danger, it is easy to depend on the world to rescue us. Read the story of Asa, king of Judah, in 2 Chronicles 16:1–10. In what ways did he *fail* to use the shield of faith to deflect the enemy's fiery darts?

By the "fiery darts of the wicked" [Eph. 6:16], Paul here refers, probably, to the temptations of the great adversary, which are like fiery darts; or those furious suggestions of evil, and excitements to sin, which he may throw into the mind like fiery darts. They are— blasphemous thoughts, unbelief, sudden temptation

to do wrong, or thoughts that wound and torment the soul.[4]

Albert Barnes

6. Satan is like a prowling enemy seeking ways to attack and destroy. He continually harasses us with his flaming missiles. What type of fiery darts do you deal with most often, and what have you found to be most effective in quenching his attacks?

Author's Reflection

One of the flaming missiles I frequently have to battle is my feeling of being totally imperfect and unworthy of God's love. I doubt His ability to mold me and use me as He pleases. Of course, the Lord wants us to recognize our poverty and consequent need of Him, but the fiery darts that Satan aims at my soul are accusations of my lack of competence and the hypocrisy in my life.

Who am I to serve in His kingdom? Look at my pride, my motives, my quick tongue—all reasons to withdraw and slink away from opportunities to serve or testify to being His child.

Like Asa, I barter with the world as I begin to depend on *my* ways of being acceptable to God and others. I will perform, I will be perfect, I will work harder, I will be strong in the power of *my* might. I must protect myself.

But this becomes a vicious cycle, for when I have faith in myself, I become *more* prideful, *more* frustrated, *more* irritable, and too tired and busy to abide under the shadow of the Almighty. I become so focused on myself and the strength I need to live daily that I forget that "He will shield [me] with his wings. He will shelter [me] with his feathers. His faithful promises are [my] armor and protection" (Ps. 91:4 NLT). I do not cry out against my Goliath as David did—"I don't need to wear anyone else's armor. I am not intimidated by your tauntings. I know that the Lord is for me, and I trust Him with all my heart."

When Hanani went to Asa, he told the king a wonderful truth: "The eyes of the LORD search the whole earth in order to strengthen those whose hearts are fully committed to him" (2 Chron. 16:9 NLT). Then he added, "What a *fool* you have been!" What a good word. How foolish to believe the lies of the enemy—to drop our guard and accept his fiery arrows. How foolish not to use the shield of faith to overcome Satan.

Yes, I am weak, imperfect, unworthy, but God has chosen to pour out His sacrificial love on me, and He asks that I take Him at His word. He desires my wholehearted faith in His ability to accomplish His purpose in my life. My trust is not in *my* faith, but in the God-given shield it becomes when I rest completely in God and His commitment to protect me. What an incredible faith-builder to know that the Lord constantly searches for any of His children who are trusting Him, so that He can strengthen their hearts to uphold their shield of faith.

> Say this: "GOD, you're my refuge.
>> I trust in you and I'm safe!"
>> That's right—he rescues you from hidden traps,
>> shields you from deadly hazards.
> His huge outstretched arms protect you—
>> under them you're perfectly safe;
>> His arms fend off all harm.
>
> *Psalm 91:2–3 The Message*

When Paul speaks of the shield of faith he is speaking of a protection which will defend the innermost life from foul and destructive invasion . . . He was not concerned with the arrangement of circumstances, but he was concerned that they should never bring disaster to his soul. He did not seek a shield to ward off ill circumstances, but he sought a shield to keep ill circumstances from doing him harm.

Paul wanted a shield against all circumstances in order that no circumstances would unman him and

impoverish the wealth of his soul. He found the shield he needed in a vital faith in Christ.[5]

John Henry Jowett

⚜

Strengthening Your Faith

Choose a Scripture from this chapter that encourages you to take up the shield of faith. Write it out here from your favorite translation, in your own words, or by personalizing it with your name. Throughout this week, meditate on your verse and pray over it as a way of accepting God's gracious protection against the enemy's attacks.

⚜Scripture Memory

Ephesians 6:16 or the verse(s) you chose to strengthen your faith.

CHAPTER 7

The Testing of Faith

I have fought a good fight, I have finished the race, and I have remained faithful.

2 Timothy 4:7 NLT

It is the "good fight of faith" and we are to have our faith tested at every round. It is a walk now from one situation to another, with opposition at every turn. Lion's dens and fiery furnaces and Goliaths will be ever in our pathway. Carnal weapons can never oppose them; it is a fight of faith.[1]

Buell H. Kazee

A test is usually given to find out what we know. From a biblical perspective, a test is given to find out what we believe. Tests in school are often stressful, and so it is in life. Trials, tests, and temptations are difficult but necessary tools in the hands of God to strengthen and prove our faith. Because God is sovereign, we endure only what He allows to enter our lives. Because He is loving, His purpose is always to do us good. Understanding that our faith will be tried for our good and for God's glory will help us perceive testing as an opportunity for growth instead of a fearful threat. "Faith must be tested," observed Oswald Chambers, "because it can be turned into a personal possession only through conflict . . . Believe steadfastly on Him and all you come up against will develop your faith."[2] How marvelous to be able to say at the end of our lives, as did Paul, "I have kept the faith."

The Purpose of Testing

1. It is easy to hope that life in this world will be hassle-free. What do these Scriptures tell us to expect?

a. Psalm 34:19

b. John 16:33

c. 2 Timothy 3:10–12

d. 1 Peter 4:12–13

2. Jesus taught that tribulation is part of living in the world. As the Lord's children who endure these testings, what should be our response to trials, and what is the desired result?

a. Romans 5:1–5

b. Hebrews 10:32–39

c. James 1:2–4

d. 1 Peter 1:3–9

3. Because we are in the world, our faith will be tried. In what area of your life do you feel that God might be testing you to strengthen your faith?

Gold is counted precious among men; faith is precious in the sight of God. Gold perisheth; faith abideth. The proof of faith is of infinitely greater importance than the proof of gold. Temptations try the Christian's faith. God tried the faith of Abraham and Job; temptation, resisted and overcome, proves faith to be real and true. And temptation refines faith; temptation borne meekly and patiently purifies faith from the taints which cling about every human character; it helps us to overcome pride and self-confidence and worldliness, and keeps us humble, distrustful of ourselves, trusting only in God. The joy of the Lord, realized amid sorrow, helps the Christian to believe that these trials, so grievous now, will be found unto praise and honour and glory at the appearing of Jesus Christ.[3]

B. C. Caffin

The Results of Testing

4. Just as God has provided armor for our trials, He has also given us assurances in His Word of His commitment to deliver us. What comfort is offered in these Scriptures?

a. 1 Corinthians 10:13

b. Hebrews 2:14–18

c. 1 Peter 5:10–11

5. The Bible vividly describes many testings of the saints—Jesus among them. For each of the following passages, summarize the test each one faced, their response, and the result of their test.

a. Genesis 22:1–19

b. Matthew 4:1–11

c. Luke 22:31–34, 54–62

6. "Tradition asserts that all his life long Peter hereafter never could hear a cock crow without falling on his knees and weeping."[4] How do you think Jesus' prayer that Peter's faith would not fail was answered?

∞

God can, in fact, use His saints' failures to strengthen their faith, which, like a tree, stands stronger for the shaking. Times of testing expose the heart's true condition. False faith, once foiled, seldom comes on again; but true faith rises and fights more valiantly, as we see in Peter. Temptation is to faith as fire is to gold. The fire not only reveals which is true gold, but makes the true gold more pure . . . Faith before temptation has much extraneous stuff that clings to it and passes for faith; but when temptation comes, the dross is discovered and consumed by the fiery trial . . . And here is all the devil gets: Instead of destroying the saint's faith, he is the means of refining it, thereby making it stronger and more precious.[5]

William Gurnall

∞

Author's Reflection

Christian or non-Christian, everyone faces trials and temptations. As God's children, though, we have a High Priest who aids us; we have armor; we have the Scriptures; and we have the promise of God that He will provide a way to escape. We have the power and choice to count it all joy when we encounter trials, knowing that the result of enduring the trial will produce a stronger faith that patiently perseveres throughout all of life.

After many years of walking with the Lord, I have experienced countless testings. I can say that with every test came the way of escape—a whispered Scripture in my heart to guide or encourage me or a check in my spirit to turn away from what I was about to do. I was given a way out, but it was always my choice whether or not to take it. If you find yourself telling God that the testing is too great or it's overwhelming you, perhaps it's a signal that you are trying to face it in your own strength instead of His. In God's mysterious way, He sets a limit on the test—God will allow only what will strengthen your faith, not tear it down, if you turn to Him for help.

Speaking of Lot, Peter wrote, "The Lord knows how to deliver the godly out of temptations" (2 Peter 2:9 NKJV). The blessing of responding righteously to a test, as Abraham did, is that it becomes easier and easier to do what is right. Choosing to trust in His faithfulness pleases God, and there is nothing to compare with His quiet voice speaking to your heart, "Well done, My good and faithful servant."

There is a wonderful promise in James 1:12: "God blesses the people who patiently endure testing. Afterward they will receive the crown of life that God has promised to those who love him" (NLT). I have no idea what the crown of life looks like, but I think I might enjoy having one! Our faith is not tested in vain—it results in honor at the revelation of Jesus Christ. God promises to reward our suffering by restoring, supporting, and strengthening us— and afterward, giving us a crown.

After Paul stated in 2 Timothy 4:7 that he had fought the good fight, he continued by affirming that a prize was awaiting: the crown of righteousness. It wasn't just for him, however, but for all who look forward eagerly to the Lord's return. And those who long for Christ's return are the ones who have remained faithful.

Faith by its very nature must be tried, and the real trial of faith is not that we find it difficult to trust God, but that God's character has to be cleared in our own minds . . . Faith in the Bible is faith in God against everything that contradicts Him—I will remain true to God's character whatever He may do. "Though He slay me, yet will I trust Him"—this is the most sublime utterance of faith in the whole of the Bible.[6]

Oswald Chambers

Strengthening Your Faith

Choose a Scripture from this chapter that helps you keep a godly perspective on testing. Write it out here from your favorite translation, in your own words, or by personalizing it with your name. Throughout this week, meditate on your verse and pray over it as a way of strengthening your faith in God's sovereign and loving purposes through trials.

✿Scripture Memory

Second Timothy 4:7 or the verse(s) you chose to strengthen your faith.

CHAPTER 8

ℱaith and ℙrayer

❧

*If you believe, you will receive whatever you
ask for in prayer.*

Matthew 21:22 NLT

But I will tell you where that faith will be born, and
grow big and lusty—in the heart of every one who goes
off quietly every day into the quiet place with the Book,
and bent knee and the bent will. Into that heart there
will come the quiet assurance that what you are asking He is doing.[1]

S. D. Gordon

$\mathscr{F}$aith permeates all of life with God, from the moment we accept His salvation through all the circumstances of daily living. It is our shield to protect us when we face trials and temptations. It is also a vitally important dimension in our prayer life. Faith is not a talisman that we wave at the throne of God, but it is crucial in shaping our intercession. Jesus praised the faith of those who approached Him to meet their needs. Matthew tells of Jesus' inability to do mighty works in Nazareth because of the unbelief there (Matt. 13:58). Understanding what the Scriptures teach about the relationship of faith and prayer is crucial for strengthening our confidence in the Lord.

Praying with Faith

1. Jesus responded to those who believed He was the Son of God, and Scripture records many instances in which He healed them. For each of the following passages, identify the need these individuals brought to Jesus, and what Jesus observed about their faith.

a. Matthew 9:20–22

b. Matthew 9:27–31

c. Matthew 15:21–28

2. The Scriptures set forth bold promises concerning answered prayer. According to these verses, what are the conditions for granting our petitions?

a. Matthew 21:18–22

b. John 14:12–13

c. James 1:5–8

d. 1 John 3:22–23

e. 1 John 5:14–15

✂

But as we have said, to pray "the prayer of faith" we must first of all study our Bibles intensely that we may know the promises of God, what they are, how large they are, how definite they are, and just exactly what is promised. In addition to that we must live so near to God, be so fully surrendered to the will of God, have such a delight in God and so feel our utter dependence upon the Spirit of God, that the Holy Spirit Himself can guide us in our prayers and indicate clearly to us what the will of God is, and make us sure while we pray that we have asked for something that is according to God's will, and thus enable us to pray with the absolute confidence that God has heard our prayer, and that "we have received" the things that we asked of Him.[2]

R. A. Torrey

Prayers of Faith

3. Although most of the Scriptures you just studied on answered prayer deal with physical healing, the majority of prayers in the Bible deal with spiritual concerns. As you read these prayers, make a list of what was on the apostle's heart for others.

a. Ephesians 3:14–19

b. Ephesians 6:18–20

c. Colossians 1:9–12

4. Paul's letters include concerns about his thorn in the flesh (which some commentators believe was a physical ailment) and others' illnesses. Summarize Paul's comments about these concerns in the following two passages.

a. 2 Corinthians 12:7–9

b. Philippians 2:25–27

c. Certainly Paul prayed with a strong faith. Why do you think the results were different in these two cases?

5. James gave specific counsel for those who suffer, those who are joyful, and those who are sick.

> a. Study James 5:13–16 and write down what he said should be done in each circumstance.

> b. What do you think this passage teaches about faith in prayer?

 ∝

Believing that we shall receive it will not force God to do something he otherwise opposes . . . Faith enough to meet the condition for such a prayer to be answered would have to come from God. When God wishes to grant a request on condition of whole-hearted belief, he himself produces that belief in the heart of his child. The faith on which the request is conditioned is no less a gift of God than is the gift which he gives to faith . . . James used strong, almost unconditional language; yet the New Testament wit-

ness as a whole is that God does not will to heal all his children of their physical afflictions. Paul certainly was a man of faith, yet his thorn in the flesh was not removed . . . James expected his readers to understand that anything he said in this passage about prayer must be taken in conjunction with what both he and other New Testament authors have to say elsewhere on the subject.[3]

C. Samuel Storms

Author's Reflection

Several years ago a precious, godly couple had a special-needs baby. They had prayed for a healthy child, but their prayer was not answered in the way they had wanted. The majority of couples we know have healthy children; we had four ourselves. I know that our prayers and our faith were no different from that of others who love God. Why is this so? Why are we told to pray in faith, and assured that our petition will be answered, when that is not always the case?

I think this issue does have everything to do with faith. What is the character of the God in whom we place our faith? What does He desire? To venture to pray requires our trust in the goodness of God. For He is loving, trustworthy, all-wise, all-knowing, full of grace and mercy. He delights that I trust Him and come to Him in faith, believing that He hears and responds.

My prayer of faith is based on wholehearted trust that I have perfect freedom to ask anything, as a child who has faith in her Father, because I love to abide in Him and His Word. However, that same faith rests in His good purposes regarding the answer I receive. It is not the amount of my faith that matters, but where my faith is placed—in a God who makes no mistakes, who is always working for the highest and best for His children. Because I seek His will and want to please Him, I want what He wants. And what He wants is that I reflect His image and depend on Him for the direction of my life.

Our friends with the special-needs child, who is now in elementary school, are facing a new test. The husband has just been diagnosed with an aggressive form of cancer. While I was visiting with the wife she commented, "I thought I could never handle having a baby who would demand so much care, but as I look back over the years I see how God has provided and given strength in such amazing ways. Now that we face this difficult trial, all I know is that God is faithful, and He will provide and sustain us."

A purified faith is a stronger faith—able to pray boldly, humbly, and submissively. Sometimes our faith can move mountains; sometimes it can only reach out and touch the hem of His garment; sometimes it simply cries out for mercy—but in all prayers of faith, in some measure, the true healing is that our eyes are opened and we see the Lord.

The faith about which Jesus and James were speaking is faith in God. It is faith in his love for us, know-

ing that he will give generously for our edification. It is faith or confidence in his wisdom, knowing that he will protect us from receiving things we pray for that would only bring us harm, things that we were unable to foresee when we prayed for them. And it is faith in his power, knowing that if what we request is in conformity with his purpose and will, he is altogether able to supply it.[4]

C. Samuel Storms

Strengthening Your Faith

Choose a Scripture from this chapter that helps you understand in a fuller way the relationship of faith and prayer. Write it out here from your favorite translation, in your own words, or personalize it with your name. Throughout this week, meditate on your verse and pray over it as a way of strengthening your faith in approaching your heavenly Father in prayer.

Scripture Memory

Matthew 21:22 or the verse(s) you chose to strengthen your faith.

CHAPTER 9

The Work of Faith

❧

This is a faithful saying, and these things I
want you to affirm constantly, that those who
have believed in God should be careful to
maintain good works. These things are good
and profitable to men.

Titus 3:8 NKJV

To trust Him means, of course, trying to do all that He
says. There would be no sense in saying you trusted a
person if you would not take his advice. Thus if you
have really handed yourself over to Him, it must follow
that you are trying to obey Him. But trying in a new
way, a less worried way. Not doing these things in order
to be saved, but because He has begun to save you already.
Not hoping to get to Heaven as a reward for your actions,
but inevitably wanting to act in a certain way because
a first faint gleam of Heaven is already inside you.[1]

C. S. Lewis

*T*he apostle Paul emphasized that faith alone enables us to receive the gift of salvation. In writing to Titus he also affirmed the value of good works in the lives of those who believe. James, the leader of the early church, described what a living, genuine faith should look like—and he emphasized that it should produce good works. Understanding the relationship between faith and good works is indispensable to becoming a woman of faith. C. S. Lewis helps us delve deeper into this understanding with his caution, "if what you call your 'faith' in Christ does not involve taking the slightest notice of what He says, then it is not faith at all—not faith or trust in Him, but only intellectual acceptance of some theory about Him."[2]

Genuine Faith

1. We cannot understand what Paul and James meant by good works apart from understanding that salvation is by faith. How do these passages explain the basis of our salvation, and the results of our salvation?

    a. Ephesians 2:8–10

    b. Titus 3:3–8

> So little inward capacity had we for such works, that we required to be created in Christ Jesus in order that we might do them. The inward new birth of the soul is indicated. When good works were required, this gracious change had to be wrought to secure them. The purpose of the new creation is to produce them . . . It is not good works first, and grace after; but grace first, and good works after.[3]
>
> *W. G. Blaikie*

2. Paul wrote that we do not receive salvation through works because if we did, we would boast of our works. Do you agree? Why?

3. Authenticity in our faith is foundational in our walk with God. What do the following verses observe about the nature of true faith?

   a. Luke 6:46–49 (See also James 1:22–25.)

b. 1 Corinthians 13:1–3

c. 1 Timothy 1:3–5

_____   _____

**It is putting an affront upon him to call him Lord,
Lord, as if we were wholly at his command, and had
devoted ourselves to his service, if we do not make
conscience of conforming to his will and serving the
interests of his kingdom.**[4]

Matthew Henry

_____   _____

4. James had much to say about an active faith and inactive
believers.

a. Summarize his teaching in James 2:14–26 concerning the
characteristics of a vital faith.

b. James insisted that good works reflect a living faith. After reading this passage, write down your understanding of some of the ways that a "living" faith is expressed.

℞

A mere profession of faith does not mean the possession of faith or the natural accompaniments of faith. Faith that is not accompanied by its inevitable and expectant fruits of faith is no faith at all. It is a mockery, and James calls such faith "dead." Moreover, Paul speaks of a true, living faith which purifies the heart and works by love (Gal. 5:6). James in this instance speaks of a profession or presumption of faith, barren and destitute of good fruit . . .

When Paul speaks of faith, he speaks of it as including the works of faith. When James speaks of faith in this instance, he speaks of false faith that does not result in the works of faith. When any apostle speaks of works resulting from faith as saving anyone, inherent in those works is included the faith that is the only way whereby those works can be produced.[5]

Spiros Zodhiates

℞

The Fruit of Faith

5. We are not left to produce the good works of faith in our own strength. What do these Scriptures teach concerning how it is possible for us to bear fruit?

a. John 15:1–5

b. 2 Corinthians 3:4–6

6. We are taught in Ephesians that we were created for good works. In the following passages, what works are we instructed to do, and what is their purpose?

a. Matthew 5:14–16

b. Titus 2:11–14

c. 1 Peter 2:11–12

— ❧ —

Everything a believer has must come from Christ, through the channel of the Spirit of grace. Just as all blessings flow to you through the Holy Spirit, nothing good can come out of you in holy thought, devout worship, or gracious act apart from the sanctifying operation of the Spirit.[6]

Charles Spurgeon

— ❧ —

Author's Reflection

One of the integral facets of my faith in God is amazement that I am His child. To have a personal relationship with my heavenly Father is certainly more than I deserve and much more than I can ever repay. His love, forgiveness, patience, and intimate personal involvement with me compel me to want to live a life pleasing to Him. My faith in a worthy Father draws me into abiding in Christ and prompts any good that I might do.

Only as I remain united with the Lord is He able to produce any fruit in my life. The few good works that evidence my faith arise from His urging, His initiating, and His encouragement, and they are for His glory. Without faith in God, my good works would be done only to bring glory to myself. It is my love and faith in a holy God, who has redeemed and purified me as His own possession, zealous for good deeds, that make the difference between living for self and living for Him.

The "good works" here refer not merely to acts of benevolence and charity, but to all that is upright and good—to an honest and holy life.[7]

Albert Barnes

Strengthening Your Faith

Choose a Scripture from this chapter that encourages you to do good works as an expression of your faith. Write it out here from your favorite translation, in your own words, or personalize it with your name. Throughout this week, meditate on your verse and pray over it as a way of strengthening yourself in the work of faith.

❧Scripture Memory

Titus 3:8 or the verse(s) you chose to strengthen your faith.

CHAPTER 10

HEROES OF THE FAITH

What is faith? It is the confident assurance
that what we hope for is going to happen. It
is the evidence of things we cannot yet see.
God gave his approval to people in days of
old because of their faith.

Hebrews 11:1–2 NLT

In Scripture there is practically no effort made to define
faith. Outside of a brief fourteen-word definition in
Hebrews 11:1, I know of no biblical definition. Even there
faith is defined functionally, not philosophically; that
is, it is a statement of what faith is in operation, not what
it is in essence. It assumes the presence of faith and shows
what it results in, rather than what it is. We will be wise
to go just that far and attempt to go no further . . . This
much is clear, and, to paraphrase Thomas à Kempis, "I
had rather exercise faith than know the definition thereof."[1]

A. W. Tozer

*I*n faith, we believe that our hope in the promise of the eternal will one day be fulfilled. The heroes of faith held on to this hope above all else, and their names—along with the evidence of their exercise of faith—are indelibly inscribed in the Word of God. A whole chapter in Hebrews is dedicated to describing and honoring these individuals who wholeheartedly trusted God. All those included in the Hebrews 11 Hall of Fame were living examples of what it means to stake your life on the promises of God. Their testimonies inspire and encourage us to abandon ourselves to the Lord. The scriptural praise these men and women receive assures us that God does reward those who diligently seek Him.

Faith Illustrated

1. Hebrews 11:1–7 sets the stage for a basic understanding of faith. Study this passage by answering the following questions.

    a. How do verses 1–3 describe the characteristics of faith?

    b. How is Abel's faith described in verse 4?

    c. What was God's response to Enoch's faith, according to verses 5–6?

d. What does verse 7 say about how Noah implemented his faith?

2. The family of Abraham is given a special section. Read Hebrews 11:8–16 and summarize why they are considered faithful.

So long as we are quietly at rest amid favorable and undisturbed surroundings, faith sleeps as an undeveloped sinew within us; a thread, a germ, an idea. But when we are pushed out from all these surroundings, with nothing but God to look to, then faith grows suddenly into a cable, a monarch oak, a master principle of life . . . It may not be necessary for us to withdraw from home and friends, but we shall have to withdraw our heart's deepest dependence from all earthly props and supports, if ever we are to learn what it is to trust simply and absolutely on the eternal God.[2]

F. B. Meyer

Faith Applied

3. The fathers of the faith and others receive special mention in Hebrews 11. After reading Hebrews 11:17–31, choose two of these heroes, read about them in the Old Testament, and write a brief paragraph about why their specific exercise of faith would please God.

a. Abraham (Gen.22:1–19)

b. Isaac (Gen. 27:27–29, with Jacob; Gen. 27:39–40, with Esau)

c. Jacob (Gen.48:8–20)

d. Joseph (Gen. 50:22–26)

e. Moses (choose only one aspect of his faith):
  • Exodus 2:1–10: his birth

  • Exodus 2:11–15: his choosing to identify with Israel

  • Exodus 12:21–28: his keeping the Passover

- Exodus 14:21–31: his crossing the Red Sea

f. Joshua (Josh. 6:1–20)

g. Rahab (Josh. 2:1–14 and 6:22–25)

4. It is encouraging to observe how different men and women expressed their faith. After reading about these diverse heroes, which person's exercise of faith most impresses you? Why?

Faith Victorious

5. The writer to the Hebrews concluded chapter 11 with a list of those whose faith accomplished various miraculous acts, and of those who were willing to sacrifice their lives for their faith. Read Hebrews 11:32–12:3.

    a. What amazing deeds were accomplished by many faithful heroes (vv. 32–35)?

    b. In what sacrificial ways did others demonstrate their faith (vv. 36–38)?

    c. As a result of studying the heroes of faith, what lesson did the writer of Hebrews want us to apply to our own lives (11:39–12:1)?

    d. Who is cited as the ultimate example of faith, and why (12:2–3)?

In time of suffering, then, pursue your course "looking unto Jesus," the perfect Example of patience; and in the presence of Gethsemane and Calvary your sufferings will appear slight, and the calm face of the supreme Sufferer will impart patience and power unto you. In seasons of despondency, when faith is weak and your spirit sinks within you, look unto Jesus, and the trust which he exercised and the destiny he attained, and let the bright example brace your heart with courage. In times of exhaustion and weariness, when you faint because of the duties and difficulties of the way, look up to Jesus and his example will raise and strengthen your powerless hands, and nerve your whole frame with new energy. And in seasons of temptation look unto him who "resisted unto blood, striving against sin," and yield not in the conflict, give no place to the tempter. Let this be our attitude, "looking unto Jesus." Let the eye of the soul be fixed upon him as our Pattern and Helper; so shall we finish our course with joy, and "receive the crown of glory that fadeth not away."[3]

W. Jones

Author's Reflection

Faith can be as straightforward as presenting a righteous offering or as monumental as building a massive ark. It can mean packing up and traveling to an unknown destination or staying in a city to wait for an attack. It can entail receiving strength to conceive a child in old age and strength to offer this same child as a sacrifice. It may lead to marching on dry land between gigantic walls of water or marching around a city for seven days. Faith can lead us unscathed from a fiery furnace or from a night of imprisonment with lions.

Faith may involve choosing to remain steadfast by enduring scourgings, imprisonment, stonings, and destitution in order to be resurrected to a better life. It means preferring to die rather than renounce God. It is believing that this world offers little in comparison to the blessing of eternity. It moves us to place everything we have in the hands of God, trusting in His promise of a heavenly country, worthy of every kind of sacrifice.

I have always been amazed by Abraham's trust in offering Isaac to God. This had to go against everything he understood about God—to take the child of promise, for whom he and Sarah had waited many long years, and lay him on the altar surely seemed a stunning reversal of everything God had said and done. Yet Abraham's confidence in God was so great that the only response from this man of faith was immediate obedience: "Abraham rose early in the morning and saddled his donkey" (Gen. 22:3 NKJV).

It pierces my heart to read that Abraham *rose early the next morning,* because over the years there have been some hard things God has asked me to do. My usual response is to wrestle and plead with God, even when He has made clear and direct requests. Recently the Lord spoke to my heart about a difficult matter. *Yes, Lord, You are right,* I responded. *I need to do that.* But I did not rise early the next morning; I purposely procrastinated, waiting for just the right time to follow through. What I was asked to do was hard, and I didn't want to do it. I was looking at my circumstances, not fixing my eyes on Jesus. I lacked faith that God would go before me and provide a "ram" for my situation.

How privileged we are to have in the Scriptures story after story of fallible human beings who became part of salvation history because they learned to rely on God's faithfulness. May we follow their example of heroic faith—to rise early the next morning and go forth trusting God.

———————————— ❧ ————————————

Faith is not a once-done act, but a continuous gaze of the heart at the Triune God.[4]

A. W. Tozer

———————————— ❧ ————————————

Strengthening Your Faith

Choose a passage from this chapter that inspires you to follow a heroic example of faith. Write it out here from your favorite translation, in your own words, or personalize it with your name. Throughout this week, meditate on your Scripture and pray over it as a way of strengthening your trust in the faithfulness of God.

❧Scripture Memory

Hebrews 11:1–2 or the verse(s) you chose to strengthen your faith.

CHAPTER 11

$\mathcal{K}$EEPING THE $\mathcal{F}$AITH

*Let's keep a firm grip on the promises that
keep us going. He always keeps his word.*

Hebrews 10:23 THE MESSAGE

Again we may fall into unbelief, doubt and disappointment because we have pinned our faith to a blessing and the blessing is lost; or to an experience and the experience vanishes; or to a person and the person fails. But true faith rests not upon a blessing, however great; or upon an experience, however deep; but upon Him through whom they came; nor does it rest upon any human exponent of victory, however sincere, but upon the Victor.[1]

Ruth Paxton

*B*ecoming a woman of faith involves growing in confidence that God is faithful. As His Spirit enables us to share in His divine nature, our faith will bear fruit. Paul listed the fruit of the Spirit in his letter to the Galatians (5:22–23), but Peter also gives us a list—seven fruits of faith. These ripen from "adding" to our faith and "guarding" it well. We are surrounded by a great cloud of witnesses who have gone before us, and it is a blessing to know they finished their race declaring their faith. Certainly we can hold fast to our hope, for our God is faithful in every way.

Holding Fast

1. B. C. Caffin commented, "Faith, St. Augustine says, is the root and mother of all virtues; St. Peter says the same."[2] Read Peter's treatment of the virtues of faith in 2 Peter 1:1–11.

a. On what basis does Peter exhort us to "add to" our faith?

b. List the qualities that Christians are to add to their faith.

c. How will these virtues help us to deepen our knowledge of the Lord?

2. These graces that are to be supplied to our faith have been compared to a symphony. They make beautiful music together; they are not intended to be cultivated alone. How do you see the importance of their relationship to one another?

If we are bringing forth the sevenfold fruit which issues out of the root of faith, we may be sure that our faith is true and living . . . The life of obedience and spiritual diligence tends to deepen continually the consciousness that the Divine power is with us, giving us all things needful for life and godliness, and so to make our calling and election sure.[3]

B. C. Caffin

3. Jude, the brother of Jesus, wrote a powerful epistle encouraging us to contend for the faith against the ungodliness of false teachers.

    a. Summarize his description of these "scoffers" (vv. 3–4, 16–19).

b. What was Jude's counsel for continuing in faith (vv. 20–23)?

God Holding Us

4. When we grasp how committed God is to us, it becomes easier to hold fast to our hope with confidence. How do these verses express the Lord's faithfulness?

a. 1 Thessalonians 5:23–24

b. 2 Thessalonians 3:3

c. 2 Timothy 2:11–13

5. Those who built on the foundation of their faith made incredible statements of their confidence in God. Read the following verses and write down the declarations these individuals made.

a. Esther 4:15–16 (Queen Esther was preparing to defy the law of the kingdom by approaching the king, unannounced and uninvited, to plead with him for her people.)

b. Job 13:15 (Job was impoverished of children, servants, and livestock, and he was suffering with painful boils.)

c. Psalm 73:25–26 (Asaph was distressed over the prosperity of the wicked, for his life was one of trouble and pain. When he went into the sanctuary of God, he gained an eternal perspective.)

d. Daniel 3:17–18 (Shadrach, Meshach, and Abed-Nego, despite the warning of death in a fiery furnace, refused to bow down and worship an image of gold.)

e. Habakkuk 3:17–19 (The prophet Habakkuk questioned God concerning evil Judah and in response, God revealed to him that the just shall live by faith; Habakkuk ended his writings with a hymn of faith.)

f. If you know of other bold declarations in the Scriptures, add to this list by writing them down here.

_____ _____

Faith is unutterable trust in God, trust which never dreams that He will not stand by us.[4]

Oswald Chambers

_____ _____

6. The heroes in Hebrews 11 and others recounted in Scripture had a firm grasp on their faith. As you think back over this study, prayerfully write out your declaration of faith so that when you are being tested or tried, you can remember your desire to honor God and to stand firm in your faith.

Author's Reflection

As I write this, there have been two major airline tragedies recently. One large airliner with hundreds of people on board inexplicably nose-dived and crashed into the ocean, and a smaller plane went down under strange circumstances, killing a popular golfer. I was interested in reading the papers to follow the questions and speculations regarding why these airplanes crashed, because I fly frequently. I could so easily imagine having been on one of those crafts.

In the aftermath of these tragedies, I was beginning to second-guess my decision to take a three-hour flight to Mexico in a single-engine plane. I was to speak at a missionary conference and a friend, who is a missionary pilot, was to fly Jack and me to Chihuahua.

Of course, at the time I was right in the middle of writing *Becoming a Woman of Faith*. The Lord seemed to be saying, "Cynthia, faith is climbing into that airplane and trusting Me with the outcome."

"Yes, Lord, but what *is* the outcome?"

"Cynthia, remember that faith concerns itself with the eternal, not the temporal. True faith rests in My faithfulness."

So again, I declared my faith: "Lord, this is Your life. I have prayed and I know that it is Your will that I make this trip. I know that You are always with me as my shield, and I know that it pleases You when I wholeheartedly abandon myself to You. My circumstances ultimately don't matter; what matters is my profound confidence in You as my loving Father. I know you desire to prove my faith so that it grows deep enough to bring praise, honor, and glory at the revelation of Jesus Christ. My heart is set on the eternal, so I will choose to walk, fly, run, wait, and rest by faith. Strengthen me to fix my eyes on Jesus so that at the end of my life I will be able to say with Paul, 'I have fought the good fight, I have finished the race, I have kept the faith.'"

O Father, may the mustard seed of my faith put down deep roots in order to endure patiently the trials I will encounter. May its trunk be strong and sturdy to deflect Satan's attacks. May this tree of faith flourish in my heart so that there is no room for doubt or fear. May its branches produce fruit that will testify to Your faithfulness. May others who see this tree be encouraged to run their race by faith alone. Lord, strengthen my faith and make it genuine, so that its leaves may shine pure gold. May my faith, which is precious to You, bring You praise and glory and honor. Amen.

Strengthening Your Faith

Choose a Scripture from this chapter that will encourage you to keep growing in faith. Write it down either in your own words, personalize it with your name, or as a special word from the Lord just to you. Throughout this week, meditate on your verse and pray over it to help you sink deep roots as a woman of faith.

❧Scripture Memory

Hebrews 10:23 or the verse(s) you chose to strengthen your faith.

Notes

Chapter 1: The Faithfulness of God

1. A. W. Tozer, *The Knowledge of the Holy* (New York: Harper & Row, 1961), 87.
2. Spiros Zodhiates, ed., *The Hebrew-Greek Key Study Bible* (Iowa Falls: World Bible Publishers, 1988), 1579.
3. Tozer, *The Knowledge of the Holy*, 87.
4. Jerry Bridges, *Trusting God* (Colorado Springs: NavPress, 1988), 197–98.
5. Charles H. Spurgeon, *The Treasury of David, Volume II* (McLean, VA: MacDonald, n.d.), 32.

Chapter 2: Encountering Doubt

1. Paul E. Little, *Know Why You Believe* (Wheaton, IL: Victor Books, 1979), 17.
2. E. R. Conder and W. Clarkson, in *The Pulpit Commentary*, ed. H. C. M. Spence and Joseph S. Excell (Peabody, MA: Hendrickson, n.d.), 23:215.

3. C. Donald Cole, *Thirsting for God* (Westchester, IL: Crossway Books, 1986), 133.

4. Matthew Henry, *Commentary on the Whole Bible* (Iowa Falls: Riverside, n.d.), 5:207–8.

5. G. K. Chesterton, *Orthodoxy* (Wheaton, IL: Harold Shaw, 1994), xiii.

Chapter 3: The Gift of God

1. R. M. Edgar, in *The Pulpit Commentary*, 20:86.

2. Oswald Chambers, in *The Oswald Chambers Daily Devotional Bible* (Nashville: Thomas Nelson, 1992), reading 128.

3. J. Radford Thomson, in *The Pulpit Commentary*, 18:22.

4. Henry, *Commentary on the Whole Bible*, 6:393.

5. Lidie H. Edmunds, "My Faith Has Found a Resting Place," in *Hymns for the Family of God* (Nashville: Paragon Associates, 1976), 75.

Chapter 4: Faith in Action

1. A. W. Tozer, *The Pursuit of God* (Camp Hill, PA: Christian Publications, 1982), 93–94.

2. Henry, *Commentary on the Whole Bible*, 4:947.

3. Chambers, *Oswald Chambers Daily Devotional Bible*, reading 222.

Chapter 5: Walking by Faith

1. Henry, *Commentary on the Whole Bible*, 6:619–20.

2. Buell H. Kazee, *Faith Is the Victory* (Dallas, TX: Crescendo Book Publications, 1972), 21.

3. Albert Barnes, *Notes on the New Testament* (Grand Rapids: Baker, 1998), 12:94.

4. J. Orr, in *The Pulpit Commentary*, 5:144.

5. Retold with permission from a seminar Lorne Sanny gave in Phoenix, Arizona, October 1999.

Chapter 6: The Shield of Faith

1. Barnes, *Notes on the New Testament*, 12:130.

2. E. W. Hengstenberg, in *The Pulpit Commentary*, 4:335.

3. William Gurnall, *The Christian in Complete Armour* (Carlisle, PA: Banner of Truth, 1986), 1:66.

4. Barnes, *Notes on the New Testament*, 12:131.

5. John Henry Jowett, quoted in *Closer Walk* (Walk Thru the Bible Ministries, 18 May 1989).

Chapter 7: The Testing of Faith

1. Kazee, *Faith Is the Victory*, 167.

2. Oswald Chambers, *My Utmost for His Highest* (Westwood, NJ: Barbour & Co., 1935), 29 August.

3. B. C. Caffin, in *The Pulpit Commentary*, 22:16–17.

4. A. Lukyn Williams, in *The Pulpit Commentary*, 15:535.

5. Gurnall, *The Christian in Complete Armour*, 1:120–21.

6. Chambers, *My Utmost for His Highest*, 31 October.

Chapter 8: Faith and Prayer

1. S. D. Gordon, *Five Laws That Govern Prayer* (New York: Fleming H. Revell, 1925), 92.

2. R. A. Torrey, *The Power of Prayer* (Grand Rapids, MI: Zondervan, 1971), 127.

3. C. Samuel Storms, *Reaching God's Ear* (Wheaton, IL: Tyndale, 1988), 123–25.

4. Ibid.

Chapter 9: The Work of Faith

1. C. S. Lewis, *Mere Christianity* (New York: Macmillan, 1952), 129.

2. Ibid.

3. W. G. Blaikie, in *The Pulpit Commentary*, 20:64.

4. Henry, *Commentary on the Whole Bible*, 5:645–55.

5. Spiros Zodhiates, *The Complete Word Study New Testament* (Chattanooga, TN: AMG Publishers, 1991), 755.

6. Charles Spurgeon, *Morning and Evening*, ed. Roy H. Clarke (Nashville: Thomas Nelson, 1994), 21 November.

7. Barnes, *Notes on the New Testament*, 12:286.

Chapter 10: Heroes of the Faith

1. Tozer, *Pursuit of God*, 87–88.

2. F. B. Meyer, *Pulpit Legends: Patriarchs of the Faith* (Chattanooga, TN: AMG Publishers, 1995), 13.

3. W. Jones, in *The Pulpit Commentary*, 21:373.

4. Tozer, *Pursuit of God*, 90.

Chapter 11: Keeping the Faith

1. Ruth Paxton, *Life on the Highest Plane* (Chicago: Moody Press, 1928), 72.

2. B. C. Caffin, in *The Pulpit Commentary*, 22:178.

3. Ibid.

4. Chambers, *My Utmost for His Highest*, 29 August.

About the Author

Cynthia Heald is an author and speaker known to many women through her best-selling Bible studies and books, including *A Woman's Journey to the Heart of God*.

A native Texan, Heald graduated from the University of Texas with a B.A. in English. She and her husband, Jack, a veterinarian by profession, are on full-time staff with The Navigators. They have four grown children and six grandchildren and reside in Tucson, Arizona.

Also by Cynthia Heald

❧

Becoming a Woman of Excellence (1986, NavPress)
Intimacy with God Through the Psalms (1987, NavPress)
Loving Your Husband (1989, NavPress)
Loving Your Wife, with Jack Heald (1989, NavPress)
Becoming a Woman of Freedom (1992, NavPress)
Becoming a Woman of Purpose (1994, NavPress)
Abiding in Christ: A Month of Devotionals (1995, NavPress)
Becoming a Woman of Prayer (1996, NavPress)
A Woman's Journey to the Heart of God (1997, Thomas Nelson)
A Journal for the Journey (1997, Thomas Nelson)
Becoming a Woman of Grace (1998, Thomas Nelson)
When the Father Holds You Close (1999, Thomas Nelson)